# ALL THINGS ANIME AND MANGA

## FANTASY, ROMANCE, AND MORE: GENRES OF ANIME AND MANGA

STUART A. KALLEN

San Diego, CA

About the Author

Stuart A. Kallen is the author of more than 350 nonfiction books for children and young adults. He has written on topics ranging from the theory of relativity to the art of electronic dance music. In 2018 Kallen won a Green Earth Book Award from the Nature Generation environmental organization for his book *Trashing the Planet: Examining the Global Garbage Glut*. In his spare time he is a singer, songwriter, and guitarist in San Diego.

© 2024 ReferencePoint Press, Inc.
Printed in the United States

**For more information, contact:**
ReferencePoint Press, Inc.
PO Box 27779
San Diego, CA 92198
www.ReferencePointPress.com

ALL RIGHTS RESERVED.
No part of this work covered by the copyright hereon may be reproduced or used in any form or by any means—graphic, electronic, or mechanical, including photocopying, recording, taping, web distribution, or information storage retrieval systems—without the written permission of the publisher.

Picture Credits:

Cover: Maxwindy/Shutterstock.com
6: Streamline Pictures/Photofest
9: Associated Press
12: NBC/Photofest
14: Destination Films/Photofest
18: Colleen Michaels/Shutterstock.com
21: Chronicle/Alamy Stock Photo
24: Free DRAWING ID/Shutterstock.com
29: Kijoiman/Shutterstock.com
32: Album/Alamy Stock Photo
35: Comedy Central/Photofest
38: Photo 12/Alamy Stock Photo
43: Cartoon Network/Photofest
45: YOSHIKI USAMI/Alamy Stock Photo
49: Usa-Pyon/Shutterstock.com
52: Album/Alamy Stock Photo
54: Colleen Michaels/Alamy Stock Photo

---

LIBRARY OF CONGRESS CATALOGING-IN-PUBLICATION DATA

Names: Kallen, Stuart A., 1955- author.
Title: Fantasy, romance, and more : genres of anime and manga / by Stuart A. Kallen.
Description: San Diego, CA : ReferencePoint Press, Inc., 2024. | Series: All things anime and manga | Includes bibliographical references and index.
Identifiers: LCCN 2023000988 (print) | LCCN 2023000989 (ebook) | ISBN 9781678205201 (library binding) | ISBN 9781678205218 (ebook)
Subjects: LCSH: Manga (Comic books)--Themes, motives--Juvenile literature. | Manga (Comic books)--Stories, plots, etc.--Juvenile literature. | Animated films--Japan--Themes, motives--Juvenile literature. | Animated television programs--Japan--Themes, motives--Juvenile literature. | Literary form--Juvenile literature. | LCGFT: Comics criticism. | Film criticism.
Classification: LCC PN6710 .K264 2024  (print) | LCC PN6710  (ebook) | DDC 741.5/952--dc23/eng/20230411
LC record available at https://lccn.loc.gov/2023000988
LC ebook record available at https://lccn.loc.gov/2023000989

# CONTENTS

## INTRODUCTION — 4
So Many Choices

## CHAPTER ONE — 8
Sci-Fi Worlds of Space and Technology

## CHAPTER TWO — 17
Romance, Drama, and Fun

## CHAPTER THREE — 27
Parodies, Slapstick, and Other Comedy

## CHAPTER FOUR — 37
Fantasy Worlds and Magic Girls

## CHAPTER FIVE — 47
Action and Adventure

Source Notes — 57
For Further Research — 60
Index — 62

# INTRODUCTION

# SO MANY CHOICES

If researchers want to study the outer limits of the human imagination, they only need to view the latest offerings from manga publishers and anime producers. Japanese comics (manga) and animated cartoons (anime) explore nearly every imaginable scenario, from high school romance to ninja battles on distant planets.

Popular manga and anime stories can be broken down into several genres. The most popular are science fiction (sci-fi), action-adventure, fantasy, romance, sports, and mystery. These genres are further divided into a dizzying number of subgenres that include martial arts, music, history, comedy, horror, detective, school, and mechanical robots, or mecha. And many popular stories combine several genres and subgenres. The popular *Akira* anime, for example, is a mash-up of sci-fi, fantasy, action-adventure, and comedy.

Hundreds of popular manga and anime stories are based on classic works of literature dropped into other genres. The cyberpunk action series *Psycho-Pass* is loosely based on the 1960s sci-fi classic *Do Androids Dream of Electric Sheep* by Philip K. Dick. The digital manga *Lore Olympus* is a reimagining of the relationships between classical Greek deities taken from stories written more than three thousand years ago. And the *Magi* series is a loose adaptation of a collection of ancient Middle Eastern folktales known as *One Thousand and One Nights*.

## SOMETHING FOR EVERYONE

In Japan manga artists are called *mangaka*. Their work can be seen in one of the more than fifty manga magazines published in Japan on a weekly, biweekly, or monthly basis. Most of these magazines serialize, or publish stories in a series; a new chapter of the story appears with each new issue. Most anime is based on serialized manga. Japan remains the main source of manga and anime that is popular on streaming channels like Crunchyroll and Netflix. However, manga and anime are also created in South Korea, the United States, and elsewhere.

Manga stories, wherever they are created, fit into five broad genres. These categories were devised long ago when publishers in Japan produced manga for specific demographic groups defined by age and gender.

In Japan most children are given *kodomo* manga as soon as they can read. The term *kodomo* comes from *kodomomuke*, which means "intended for children." Most of the manga in this category, such as *Hello Kitty* and *Doraemon*, is created for kids under age ten.

*Shonen* means "young male" in Japanese. Shonen manga is therefore aimed at boys aged ten to eighteen. Some of the most popular manga and anime series, such as *One Piece* and *Dragon Ball Z*, first appeared in shonen magazines. Nicole Rousmaniere, professor of Japanese arts at England's University of East Anglia, says of the shonen genre, "The graphic action scenes and riveting story lines that develop through multiple instalments help to make this form addictive."[1] Manga and anime for males aged fifteen to twenty-four is categorized as *seinen*. This genre features complex, violent, sexual stories like those found in *Berserk* and *Ghost in the Shell*.

Manga and anime for female readers aged twelve to eighteen is known as *shojo*, which translates as "young girl." While shonen stories

> "The graphic action scenes and riveting story lines that develop through multiple instalments [of shonen manga] help to make this form addictive."[1]
>
> —Nicole Rousmaniere, professor of Japanese arts at the University of East Anglia

tend to focus on fighting and conquest, shojo features romance, love triangles, fractured friendships, and drama. Some of the most popular stories in the shojo genre include *Sailor Moon* and *Ouran High School Host Club*. The adult version of shojo, called *josei*, was created for women aged eighteen to forty. Popular series like *Loveless* and *Honey and Clover* are similar to American soap operas on television.

Most manga and anime genres share common elements. Stories tend to focus on a central character, or protagonist, who is on a personal quest. Collectively, these heroes are often adolescent underdogs who need to master various skills to succeed. Central characters are often forced to confront their own weaknesses. They must master their emotions, overcome personal limitations, expand the bonds of friendship, and grow. Such story elements apply to protagonists whether they are orphaned aliens, trans-

*Popular manga and anime stories fall into several genres. Some, such as* Akira *(a scene from which is shown here), are a mash-up of science fiction, fantasy, action-adventure, and comedy.*

forming robots, or reincarnated magicians. Anime reviewer Madison Roach writes, "A huge element of interest for people is the ability to relate to the main protagonist of the story, who's almost always human in some aspect."[2]

## THOUSANDS OF SHOWS

Millions of people are tuning in to watch their favorite genres on streaming services. The data analysis organization World Population Review says approximately 72 percent of people in the United States watch anime regularly. And in 2022 Netflix estimated that there were more than 100 million anime viewers worldwide. That is about one out of every eighty people on earth. Creators have to produce enough stories to satisfy the demand. Netflix alone announced it was launching forty new anime titles in 2022. Crunchyroll offers its 5 million subscribers access to sixteen thousand hours of programming and more than forty-four thousand episodes. Visitors to the Crunchyroll website can browse anime by subgenres that include magical girls, thriller, idols, and postapocalyptic.

Each year, more than eight thousand manga stories are printed in Japan, and hundreds more are turned into anime. With no end in sight, artists and writers will continue to explore the furthest reaches of the imagination to meet the demand for this unique form of entertainment.

## CHAPTER ONE

# SCI-FI WORLDS OF SPACE AND TECHNOLOGY

In 2022 anime fans flocked to theaters across North America to participate in Crunchyroll Movie Night. The anime selected for the event was the feature-length sci-fi extravaganza *Mobile Suit Gundam: Cucuruz Doan's Island*. The anime, which is part of the *Mobile Suit Gundam* franchise, has all the elements of a gripping sci-fi tale. It combines real science, space travel, robots, and fearsome futuristic weaponry. The story pits soldiers of the Earth Federation against space rebels from another planet. The federation fighters battle enemies wearing mecha, mechanical robot suits that are referred to as Gundam. Anime journalist Charles Solomon describes the mecha as "a fusion of an outsized space suit, a one-man spaceship and a set of samurai [warrior] armor."[3] The death-dealing war machines are piloted by young psychic soldiers, including the fearless teenager Amuro Ray. The anime has plenty of fiery explosions and drawn-out battles with mecha pilots wielding laser swords and axes.

## ROBOT INNOVATORS

The eye-popping mecha battles in *Cucuruz Doan's Island* were created using computer-generated imagery (CGI) software. The 3-D effects made the robot combat seem to pop off the screen. But even as viewers enjoyed the dynamic visuals created by the latest computer technology, the basic plot of the anime can be traced back to a distant era. The original *Mobile Suit Gundam* was a television series created in 1979 by mecha and anime innovator Yoshiyuki Tomino. In the decades that followed, Tomino's *Gundam* franchise grew to include more than 750 TV anime episodes and more than a dozen full-length movies, along with a manga series and a number of video games. *Gundam* model kits also proved to be extremely popular; more than 714 million character and vehicle models from the *Gundam* universe have been sold since the kits were first introduced in 1980.

*Mecha and anime innovator Yoshiyuki Tomino created the original* Mobile Suit Gundam *as a television series in 1979. The* Gundam *franchise eventually grew to include hundreds of television anime episodes, more than a dozen full-length movies, a manga series, and a number of video games.*

Tomino began his career in 1964 as an artist and illustrator on one of the earliest Japanese anime series, *Tetsuwan Atomu* (*Mighty Atom* in English). The story's protagonist is a little robot known as Mighty Atom. He first appeared in a manga series created by Osamu Tezuka in 1952. Mighty Atom has a nuclear reactor heart, a computer brain, searchlight eyes, a machine gun on his back side, lasers in his hands, and rockets in his feet, which allows him to fly. He can understand sixty languages, has super hearing and vision, and easily smashes through concrete with his 100,000-horsepower strength. Despite his awesome powers, Mighty Atom is also cute and lovable.

The sci-fi genre was not new in the 1950s, but Tezuka's artistic style was unique. Instead of creating a comic strip with flat figures in square boxes, Tezuka used a cinematic drawing technique that featured panels that unfolded like a movie. Tezuka created scenes that zoomed in from a distance to extreme close-ups that might show only lines of emotion in a character's eyes and forehead. Some pages contained a series of wide panels that took in an entire landscape. These scenes were meant to remind readers of a movie camera panning from side to side. Another technique showed the action from above, below, and unusual angles.

Tezuka deliberately broke with the past when he created *Mighty Atom*. He felt traditional comics, which were drawn as if an audience were watching action on a stage, were stale and boring. "This [old style of drawing] made it impossible to create dramatic or psychological effects," he said. "I experimented with close-ups and different angles, and instead of using only one frame for an action scene or the climax (as was customary), I made a point of depicting a movement or facial expression with many frames, even many pages. The result was a super-long comic."[4]

## SETTING THE STYLE

*Mighty Atom* was incredibly popular; the manga was serialized for sixteen years. In 1963 the lovable Mighty Atom starred in Japan's first televised anime series. The series was exported

## ROBOTS AND MORE ROBOTS

The *Mighty Atom* manga, which debuted in 1952, helped launch the entire robot genre. In 1956 mangaka (manga artist) Mitsuteru Yokoyama created a giant mechanical monster called *Tetsujin 28-gō*, literally *Iron Man #28*. The 25-ton (22.7 metric ton), 92-foot-tall (28 m) mecha flies with a rocket pack on his back. Like many mecha manga to follow, the hulking machine was operated by a kid—in this case a ten-year-old boy named Shotaro Kaneda, who used a remote control to move Iron Man. The Iron Man manga was adapted into four different anime TV series, the first of which was exported to the United States in 1964 as *Gigantor*.

In 1972 the mangaka Go Nagai created *Mazinger Z*, the first monster robot with its own onboard pilot, a young man named Koji Kabuto. The *Mazinger Z* anime was first shown in the United States in 1977. The series featured lovable supporting characters, including Sayaka Yumi, the female robot pilot. Nagai also introduced a funny robot, Boss Borot, made from worn-out parts and old garbage. In the United States *Mazinger Z* was the inspiration for the 1980s show *The Transformers*. This extremely popular animated TV series depicted a war among giant robots that could transform into vehicles, animals, and other objects.

to the United States and renamed *Astro Boy*. From 1963 to 1965 over one hundred episodes of *Astro Boy* were shown on NBC on Sunday mornings. The original Japanese dialogue was dubbed into English.

*Mighty Atom* was produced at the animation studio called Mushi Production, founded by Tezuka in 1961. Anyone watching the original episodes of *Astro Boy* on YouTube can see how Tezuka's distinct artistic animation style became as widely influential as his manga drawing techniques. To save time and money, Tezuka created what is called limited animation.

With limited animation, characters have a restricted range of motion; at times they freeze on the screen in a dramatic pose. Sometimes their hairdo might be the only thing that moves in a frame. While American animators use at least a dozen different mouth movements when characters speak, anime characters are often drawn with only three mouth positions: open, shut, and half-open. Sometimes characters speak with their back to the viewer, so no animation is necessary. This style is still popular, even alongside modern anime created with CGI.

More than one hundred episodes of the anime series Astro Boy *were shown on NBC from 1963 to 1965.*

The artistic style of *Mighty Atom* remains part of this art form today. Modern characters still have huge eyes that often fill the screen when they express their emotions. When they cry, rivers of tears flow from their eyes, and when they are in trouble, sweat pours off their faces. These and other elements derive from Tezuka's style.

## SPACE COWBOYS

*Astro Boy* inspired several other sci-fi anime series that were shown in the United States in later years, including *Gigantor* and *Mazinger Z*. But in the United States, as well as Japan, popular anime received little respect from reviewers, who continued to think of the cartoons as children's entertainment. Shinichirō Watanabe, who grew up on Tezuka's manga and anime, wanted to change this perception. This desire led him to direct the sci-fi anime series *Cowboy Bebop*, with twenty-six episodes that originally ran on Japanese TV from 1998 to 1999.

*Cowboy Bebop* chronicles the escapades of ragtag bounty hunters, known as Cowboys. The Cowboys—Spike Spiegel, Jet Black, and Faye Valentine—explore the universe in a spaceship called *Bebop*, a broken-down craft that looks outdated. This fits with the overall theme of *Cowboy Bebop*, which is based on the genre known as film noir, popular in the 1950s. The film noir genre features menacing criminals and a dark, moody visual style. Another mid-century element can be found in the soundtrack; wild, improvisational bebop jazz music from the 1940s plays during the story's numerous mecha battles, fist fights, and explosions. *Cowboy Bebop* also mixes in tropes from the American western cowboy genre; the protagonists travel to lawless frontier towns filled with swaggering outlaws and bounty hunters who make a living capturing criminals.

*Cowboy Bebop* was the first anime ever broadcast on Cartoon Network's Adult Swim programming block. That started in 2001. Reruns of the show have aired on Cartoon Network for thirteen years, drawing legions of new fans to the series. With its long-running popularity *Cowboy Bebop* received credit for introducing anime to a new generation of Western viewers. Tech journalist Monica Kim writes, "[Fans] loved the jazz and blues-inspired soundtrack, the elegant film noir style, and existential themes [boredom, loneliness]. . . . It's been called one of the greatest anime series of all time, and it is arguably the single most popular 'serious' anime among Americans."[5]

> "In Japan it was widely understood that Cowboy Bebop was lightning in a bottle—that it was a fantastic synergy of creative talent that you couldn't explain."[6]
>
> —Jonathan Clements, anime journalist

The original *Cowboy Bebop* was still streaming on Netflix and Crunchyroll in 2023. The series' long run is held up as an example of a great story with unique qualities that continues to attract new fans. Anime journalist Jonathan Clements explains the show's popularity: "In Japan it was widely understood that *Cowboy Bebop* was lightning in a bottle—that it was a fantastic synergy of creative talent that you couldn't explain."[6]

*In the anime series* Cowboy Bebop, *a ragtag group of bounty hunters named Spike Spiegel, Jet Black, and Faye Valentine explore the universe in a broken down, outdated-looking spaceship.*

## THE SCIENCE OF DR. STONE

Like many other sci-fi anime, *Cowboy Bebop* is also classified as postapocalyptic. Stories in the postapocalyptic subgenre take place in settings in which civilization is crumbling or has already collapsed. Most humans have been killed by a catastrophic event such as a nuclear war, plague, or alien invasion. Postapocalyptic worlds might be ruled by robots, bloodthirsty barbarians, or any manner of mind-boggling monsters.

The binge-worthy anime *Dr. Stone* is classified as a postapocalyptic sci-fi series. The anime is based on a manga written by Riichiro Inagaki and illustrated by the South Korean artist Boichi. Serialized from 2017 to 2022, *Dr. Stone* features real science. The complicated concepts are delivered by the protagonist, Senku Ishigami, a fifteen-year-old science prodigy. *Dr. Stone* begins in the year 2038, when a mysterious flash of green light turns all animals and humans, including Senku, to solid stone. Senku awakens thirty-seven hundred years in the future.

Senku discovers his return to life was aided by a nitric acid solution dripping from the roof of a cave. Sometimes the action pauses for Senku to conduct science experiments for viewers. In one example, he shows how nitric acid can be mixed with distilled alcohol to make a fluid that can etch metals. Senku also discusses what kind of mushrooms are edible, how to preserve foods, and how to mix concrete. Reviewer Arius Raposas writes, "*Dr. Stone* may have a number of experiments children should not really try at home, but this was nonetheless an exceptional example of using entertainment . . . for scientific education."[7]

Senku concocts a nitric acid formula that can crack the stone encasing petrified humans. This allows him to pursue his dream of creating a new civilization called the Kingdom of Science. In this kingdom scientists are the leaders, while strong people do all the work. Senku revives his muscle-bound but not-too-smart

> "*Dr. Stone* may have a number of experiments children should not really try at home, but this was nonetheless an exceptional example of using entertainment . . . for scientific education."[7]
>
> —Arius Raposas, reviewer

## BOICHI AND SOUTH KOREAN SCI-FI

The South Korean artist Boichi illustrated the popular *Dr. Stone* manga, which was turned into an equally popular anime. Boichi wanted to become a manga artist at an early age. This led him to major in physics in college so he could better understand the science aspects of science fiction. While Boichi lives and works in Japan, he remains a huge fan of South Korean sci-fi *manhwa* (the Korean word for "manga").

South Korean sci-fi covers many of the same themes found in Japanese manga, including robots, space exploration, time travel, and parallel universes. Protagonists are usually young adults who are tasked with saving the world. But some manhwa stories are even darker and scarier than those found in manga. *City of Blank*, created by an artist known as 66, is about a world where ghostlike entities called Blanks can steal anyone's face at any time. *Duty After School*, by Ha Il-Kwon, follows a student club in which extracurricular activities include fighting vicious enemies in a major war. The popularity of manhwa in every genre is growing worldwide, thanks to South Korean apps like Webtoon and Netcomics, which present full-color comics formatted for the small screens on cell phones.

best friend, Taiju Oki. He also brings back a famous martial artist named Tsukasa Shishiō. Tsukasa establishes a faction of survivors called Stone World that eventually battles Senku's Kingdom of Science. This theme of brains versus brawn is common to many stories, but it is the environment, the science, and the interesting characters in *Dr. Stone* that makes this narrative engaging.

The art in *Dr. Stone* is visually stunning. The anime's pastoral world features multiple hues of green and brown, while the sky and clouds are portrayed in spectacular shades of blue, purple, and pink. In 2019 the combination of visual beauty and engaging plotlines landed *Dr. Stone* on the Crunchyroll list called Top 25 Best Anime of the 2010s. After two well-received seasons, it was announced that season three of *Dr. Stone* would premiere in 2023. The manga series is also very popular; *Dr. Stone* was compiled in paperback books called *tankōbon* in Japan. These books contain multiple chapters of a single series. The twenty-six volumes of *Dr. Stone* tankōbon had sold over 13 million copies by 2022.

The high-quality production values of recent sci-fi anime like *Dr. Stone* are worlds apart from *Mighty Atom* and *Gigantor*. But science, technology, and futuristic machines have remained a staple of the sci-fi genre. And like science fiction in any medium, most stories in manga and anime feature dire warnings about the misuse of technology. Characters often use science for evil purposes or become mad with power, leading to catastrophic results. And stories like *Cowboy Bebop* demonstrate that living in a futuristic world of high-tech gadgets and space travel does not translate into human happiness.

People have long been fearful of the unintended consequences associated with technology. Sci-fi manga and anime allow fans a glimpse into the unknown to see how robots, artificial intelligence, spaceships, and mecha can be used for good or bad purposes. By posing big questions about human motivations and desires, the fiction in science fiction allows people to view the real world in a new way.

## CHAPTER TWO

# ROMANCE, DRAMA, AND FUN

The romantic comedy *Fruits Basket* has a long and interesting history. The manga series created by Natsuki Takaya was first serialized in 1998 in the Japanese shojo magazine *Hana to Yume* (*Flowers and Dreams*). While the series was initially popular in Japan, *Fruits Basket* became an international phenomenon when the English-language manga was published in the United States in 2006. As reporter Coco Masters wrote about the creator of the series at the time, "[Natsuki Takaya has] become one of the industry's top shojo authors, creating manga for women that now sell in bookstores across the globe."[8]

*Fruits Basket* combines romance with the supernatural. The popular series follows high school student Tohru Honda after her mother dies in a car accident. Tohru moves in with her classmate Yuki Sohma, only to discover that his wealthy family lives with a curse. The thirteen members of the family are possessed by spirits of the Chinese zodiac, represented by animals such as the rat, ox, tiger, snake, monkey, dog, and dragon. The characters in the manga turn into zodiac animals when hugged by members of the opposite sex. Tohru tries to break the curse and ends up changing the family forever.

*Fruits Basket* has many moments of drama. The story depicts serious emotional issues such as suicide, depression,

> "As a pillar of the shōjo genre of romance, comedy, and drama in anime and manga, *Fruits Basket* is a reputable classic."[10]
>
> —Callie Cadorniga, anime reviewer

and parental abuse. But there are also moments of lighthearted fun, magic, and mystery. As manga reviewer Deb Aoki writes, "*Fruits Basket* starts off as a goofy romantic comedy, then develops into an emotional roller coaster that mixes humor, fantasy, profoundly emotional romance and family drama for an addictive mix that has made it the best-selling *shojo manga*."[9]

*Fruits Basket* was adapted into a twenty-six-episode anime that first appeared on Japanese television in 2001. Although the original anime was never shown on American television, it was released in the United States on DVD in 2007. And the story had such lasting popularity that the entire manga was adapted to a second anime series by Crunchyroll in 2019. Anime reviewer Callie Cadorniga attests, "As a pillar of the shōjo genre of romance, comedy, and drama in anime and manga, *Fruits Basket* is a reputable classic."[10]

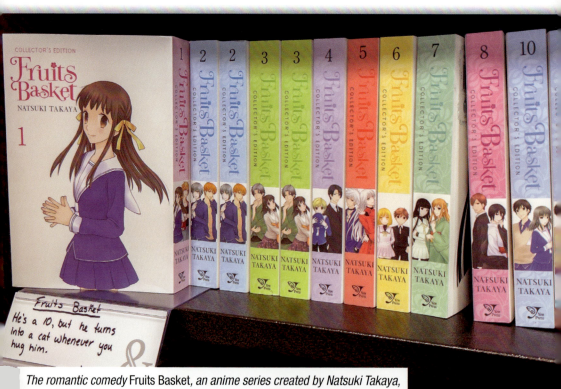

The romantic comedy Fruits Basket, an anime series created by Natsuki Takaya, was initially only popular in Japan but became an international phenomenon when the English-language manga was published in the United States in 2006.

## FEMALE MANGAKA

Takaya has said in interviews that she decided to become a mangaka in 1979 when she was just six years old. At the time she made that decision, the world of shojo manga was rapidly changing in Japan. While shojo manga had been published in various magazines since the 1920s, most stories were written and illustrated by men. Protagonists in romance stories were often unloved tomboys or helpless waifs who would only find happiness through marriage.

By the early 1970s the popularity of manga was rapidly growing in Japan. This created intense competition among publishers to attract loyal female readers aged eight to eighteen. To better capture female sensibilities, publications like *Shōjo Comic* and *Nakayoshi* (*Best Friend*) hired female artists, including Yumiko Oshima, Riyoko Ikeda, Moto Hagio, and others. The switch to female artists and writers helped increase sales of shojo manga. Because many of the new artists were around twenty-four years old, newspaper articles about the rise of female mangaka referred to this new generation of artists as the *Showa 24* (Year 24 Group) or the Magnificent 24s.

## EXPLORING NEW TOPICS

Female mangaka created works in many genres, but the most popular series were melodramatic romances or romances combined with other genres such as supernatural stories or vampire tales. The series *The Rose of Versailles*, created by Riyoko Ikeda in 1972, is a historical romance with a twist. The story takes place in France in the 1780s, before the French Revolution. It chronicles the lives of two women, Marie Antoinette, the queen of France, and Oscar François de Jarjayes, a cross-dressing girl raised as a boy. *The Rose of Versailles* was the first shojo manga story to achieve widespread popularity in Japan, selling more than 20 million tankōbon. The series was later adapted as an anime, a musical play, and a live-action film.

## AN ARTISTIC REVOLUTION

Female manga creators from the Year 24 Group revolutionized the artistic styles seen in shojo magazines. And the stylistic changes they pioneered continue to play a prominent visual role in modern manga and anime. These artists filled pages with rays of light, beautiful trees, and wafting leaves. Flowers were used freely to symbolize the moods and thoughts of characters. When the lotus flower appears on the page or the screen, it represents purity of body, speech, and mind. Cherry blossoms are associated with loyalty, roses with sensuality, and irises with strength, vitality, boldness, and power.

The artists drew facial close-ups that filled an entire page. Feelings were expressed with dark wavy lines or a stream of exploding psychedelic lightning bolts. Female characters were drawn with huge, round, doll-like eyes and extremely long eyelashes. As Japanese art and culture expert Mizuki Takahashi writes, "Starry eyes symbolize the love and dreams of the characters. . . . [They] also serve as mirrors that reflect the character's emotions. The eyes literally are the windows of the soul; by looking at the eyes, the readers can intuit the character's feelings, which remain unexpressed in dialog."

Quoted in Mark W. MacWilliams, ed., *Japanese Visual Culture*. Armonk, NY: East Gate, 2008, p. 124.

Ikeda and other female mangaka were fearless when it came to exploring the sexuality of characters (without including explicit sex). *The Rose of Versailles* features romantic love between the two female protagonists, something that was considered taboo at the time. Another romance manga series from that era, *The Heart of Thomas* by Moto Hagio, is about a suicidal gay teenager who must hide his feelings. These themes, which were ignored by male mangaka, helped normalize gay romance and other same-sex issues in mainstream shojo.

Over the years so many manga and anime series have been created with gay characters that the topic is no longer considered shocking. Manga and anime with lesbian women are referred to as *yuri*, or "girls' love." The romantic genre featuring gay males is referred to as *yaoi*, or "boys' love." Boys' love is largely created by women for female consumers. According to data from the Yano Research Institute, more than 60 percent of boys' love fans are heterosexual females aged fifteen to twenty-nine. Journalist Kirsty Kawano explains the attraction: "The obstacles to [boys' love] characters . . . are much higher than in regular narratives, which consequently makes the stories more romantic, or satisfyingly heartrending for readers."[11]

> "The obstacles to [boys' love] characters . . . are much higher than in regular narratives, which consequently makes the stories . . . satisfyingly heartrending for readers."[11]
>
> —Kirsty Kawano, journalist

## HISTORICAL ROMANCE

*The Rose of Versailles* was one of the first manga to spike interest in historical romances. Some fans of the series went on to study French and visit the Palace of Versailles in France, where the story takes place. Historical romances remain popular, and fans of the subgenre can find stories set in almost every era from ancient China to twentieth-century America. The manga romance *Emma* by Kaoru Mori transpires in nineteenth-century London. The basic plot has been used in countless other romance manga and anime. Emma is a hardworking housemaid who falls in love with a handsome, wealthy young man. His family strongly disapproves of the relationship and tries to end it. The twists and turns of this

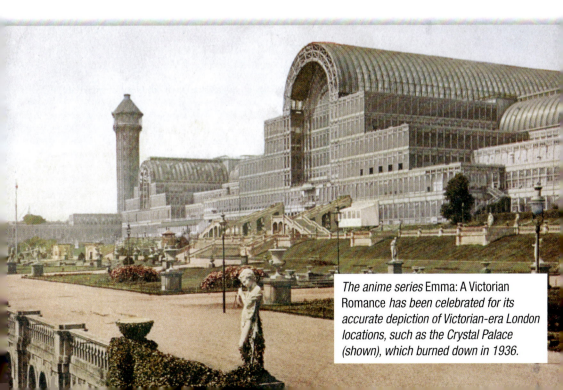

*The anime series* Emma: A Victorian Romance *has been celebrated for its accurate depiction of Victorian-era London locations, such as the Crystal Palace (shown), which burned down in 1936.*

story have provided enough drama for twenty-four anime episodes renamed *Emma: A Victorian Romance.* The anime has been celebrated for accurately depicting Victorian-era London locations, including King's Cross railway station, Covent Garden, and the Crystal Palace.

Some historical romances are less realistic, but they tie in other subgenres to provide an unexpected turn of events. *Yona of the Dawn* by mangaka Mizuho Kusanagi includes adventure, fantasy, and supernatural elements. The story unfolds in a historical setting that combines features of early Japanese, Korean, and Chinese cultures. Sixteen-year-old Yona is a princess in the fictional kingdom of Kouka. Like many female characters in manga and anime, Yona is innocent and sheltered. She grew up in a castle, where she was protected from the outside world. And, as with so many stories, the naive teenager must save the world. Yona sets out on a long journey to raise an army that will fight for the survival of her kingdom. She must gain confidence and strength and learn to use weapons to defend herself. While dodging swords and fists, Yona must deal with the romantic tension between herself and her bodyguard, Hak. Numerous unsuitable suitors appear in Yona's life on a regular basis.

## TOO MANY ADMIRERS

*Yona of the Dawn* has elements of another subgenre known as harem. The harem category was introduced in the 1990s and rapidly attracted an audience. The original stories featured male protagonists who were pursued by three or more female suitors. Eventually, reverse-harem stories like *Yona of the Dawn* were created. In this subgenre a female protagonist has many male admirers.

Whatever the gender balance, the protagonists in most harem stories are very nice but clueless about the romantic intentions of the other characters. Sometimes the suitors are not all the same gender, as in the popular harem anime *Kiss Him, Not Me*. The story, created by the female mangaka known as Junko, was serialized from 2013 to 2018; the anime adaptation was first shown on Crunchyroll in 2016.

## POPULAR ANIME WITH LGBTQ+ CHARACTERS

In the 1970s female manga artists introduced LGBTQ+ characters to manga readers for the first time. While Japanese society emphasizes traditional conservative social mores, shojo that realistically portray a wide range of romantic relationships became extremely popular without creating much controversy. Today gay, trans, and nonbinary characters are often seen in manga and anime.

Almost all the characters in the 2019 boys' love musical romance *Given* identify as LGBTQ+. The anime, based on a long-running manga by Natsuki Kizu, follows four high school students in a rock band who have a series of romantic relationships. *Attack on Titan*, based on a manga series created by Hajime Isayama, features two female characters who are in love. The story, about a world where people must fight human-devouring titans, also has a nonbinary character who does not present as male or female. The popular anime series *My Hero Academia* and *Hunter x Hunter* both have characters who identify as trans. Most LGBTQ+ series are considered family friendly because they focus on the give and take of romantic relationships rather than on sex. And during Gay Pride Month every June, these series are featured in special promotions on Crunchyroll, the Cartoon Network, and other media.

In *Kiss Him, Not Me*, the female protagonist, Kae Serinuma, is an *otaku*, a Japanese word that describes someone who has an obsessive interest in manga and anime. Kae has four attractive young men hoping to date her, and one young woman named Shima. Kae is attracted to Shima but she fantasizes about the young men getting together with one another in romantic relationships. The story features bright colors, humorous, over-the-top character reactions, and laugh-out-loud situations. The premise of this light romantic comedy might seem shocking to some, but as anime reviewer Jitendar Canth writes, "*Kiss Him, Not Me* is a delightful show that has an important message about acceptance and tolerance beneath the usual relationship hijinks. The characters fall for Kae Serinuma based on physical attraction at first, but they quickly accept her for who she is, rather than try to change her."[12]

> "*Kiss Him, Not Me* is a delightful show that has an important message about acceptance and tolerance beneath the usual relationship hijinks."[12]
>
> —Jitendar Canth, anime reviewer

## YOUNG IDOLS

Romantic competition between colorful characters can be found in the subgenre referred to as idol. These stories revolve around dazzling young people in good-looking outfits who struggle desperately to become pop music idols. Protagonists face off against snooty rivals while dealing with other obstacles such as sickness or injuries that prevent them from making it to the top. Themes in the idol subgenre dwell on the importance of teamwork, friendship, and dedication to one's dreams. The anime stories feature plenty of music, including rock, pop, hip-hop, show tunes, and heavy metal.

*Skip Beat!* is one of the longest-running and most widely appreciated series in the idol subgenre. Created by mangaka Yoshiki Nakamura in 2002, the story had more than 280 chapters by 2022,

Generations of mangaka have found clever, artistic ways to explore the basic human pursuit of love in all its heartwarming, horrifying, heartrending, and hilarious forms.

compiled into forty-eight tankōbon. The manga was published in the United States in 2006, and the twenty-five-episode anime first appeared on Crunchyroll in 2008 and was still available in 2023.

*Skip Beat!* is the story of Kyoko Mogami, a sixteen-year-old girl who hangs around with her childhood crush, a boy named Shotaro Fuwa who is seeking pop idol stardom. Kyoko works as a maid to support Shotaro as he pursues his dreams. Kyoko overhears a conversation between Shotaro and his manager. Shotaro admits Kyoko is boring and plain and that he is only using her for financial support until he finds fame. Kyoko vows revenge. She decides to become a bigger star than Shotaro. Episodes follow Kyoko as she navigates the show business world filled with love, hated rivals, talented troublemakers, and coldhearted businessmen. Kyoko eventually discovers that she loves singing and acting and gives up her dreams of revenge on Shotaro. Anime journalist Sebastian Stoddard says *Skip Beat!* "has become beloved by fans inside and outside idol anime circles for its story and characters, which holds up as a staple of the genre."[13]

## SINGING ZOMBIES

The idol category is sometimes combined with other subgenres. One of the strangest idol subgenres mixes in horror, or as reviewer Raziel Reaper puts it, "they replaced all cute girls with cute zombie girls."[14] The story of *Zombie Land Saga* begins in 2008, when one of the cute girls, Sakura Minamoto, is run over by a truck on her way to an audition. Ten years later, Sakura is brought back to life by a manic music producer who is also a necromancer, a magician who can raise the dead. Sakura joins six other deceased girls to form a zombie idol group called Franchouchou. While the plot might seem bleak, the show relies on dark comedy to poke fun at the entire Japanese idol industry.

Even within the comedy-horror genre mash-up, *Zombie Land Saga* characters deal with heartbreak, jealousy, anxiety, and low self-esteem, problems often suffered by aspiring idols in the real world. But the series about undead idols does not dwell on the negative. And the catchy music, which includes rock, soft ballads, and even rap battles, adds another entertaining element to the series that helped make *Zombie Land Saga* one of the most popular anime on Crunchyroll from 2018 to 2021.

## OLD STORIES WITH NEW CONCEPTS

Most romantic manga and anime stories, whatever the subgenres, are filled with stereotypical characters, including icy beauties, sassy girlfriends, super-genius schoolboys, dumb tough guys, and rich male heartthrobs. Female protagonists are often rejected by their families. The young women are poor and plain but with big hearts and good intentions. While some criticize these tropes, they have long been a staple of books, plays, movies, and TV shows across many cultures. As with manga and anime, the most popular Hollywood stories are based on the old cliché: boy meets girl; boy loses girl; boy and girl are reunited for a happy ending. Romantic manga and anime simply tap into these most universal of struggles: seeking love, finding romance, and experiencing heartbreak.

Within the romance genre framework generations of mangaka have found clever, artistic ways to explore the basic human pursuit of love. And as the continual flood of romance manga and anime stories prove, love is in the air—and on the air—in all its heartwarming, horrifying, heartrending, and hilarious forms.

## CHAPTER THREE

# PARODIES, SLAPSTICK, AND OTHER COMEDY

One-Punch Man is a nerdy guy whose real name is Saitama. He is the protagonist of *One-Punch Man* manga and anime, and he has a superpower. Saitama can defeat any enemy with a single punch. But One-Punch Man is bored. Although the superhero lives in a world filled with a crazy assortment of cyborgs, hybrid animal monsters, and mad genius outlaws, he cannot find an opponent who can withstand his punching power. This leaves Saitama with one wish: to find an enemy strong enough to challenge him.

Saitama does not resemble the dazzling superheroes that populate his world. Other high-ranking heroes—with names like Blast, Flashy Flash, and Atomic Samurai—look like crime-fighting crusaders. They have showy moves, magnificent outfits, and flowing hair. Saitama is skinny, bald, and plain looking. He is unemployed and struggles to pay the rent on his tiny one-room apartment. When duty calls, Saitama will take time off from his boring life to save the world from fearsome monsters. But no one seems to notice his feats. Even those he fights do not know who he is.

> "There are tons of tropes and clichés normally found in superhero and shonen stories that *One-Punch Man* subverts and pokes fun at."[15]
>
> —Rafael Motamayor, anime reviewer

While Saitama might be frustrated with the lack of thrills in his life, fans of the series love his absurd story. *One-Punch Man* delivers plenty of action while comically skewering the superhero genre. Villains are amusingly incompetent, other crime fighters are vain and foolhardy, and even the direst moments might be interrupted by a wisecrack from Saitama. Anime reviewer Rafael Motamayor remarks, "There are tons of tropes and clichés normally found in superhero and shonen stories that *One-Punch Man* subverts and pokes fun at."[15]

The creator of *One-Punch Man* is an average guy, much like his protagonist. He was an unknown mangaka with the mysterious moniker One who self-published a crudely drawn manga as a digital webcomic in 2009. Webcomics, also called web manga, are made to be viewed on a computer, tablet, or smartphone. They appear on-screen as printed manga magazines with multiple frames of black-and-white drawings on each page. Readers flip through the pages as if they were reading a digital book.

*One-Punch Man* was instantly popular, receiving millions of hits and comments within months. The manga was picked up by the online magazine Jump Comics in 2012, and the series was adapted to anime in 2015. *One-Punch Man* received a 100 percent approval rating by the review website Rotten Tomatoes. When Crunchyroll began streaming *One-Punch Man* in 2019, it quickly became one of site's most-watched anime series.

## THE POWERS OF MOB

Humor is an often-overlooked category of manga and anime, but almost all stories, no matter how serious, feature moments of comic relief. Manga and anime creators often get laughs with silly facial expressions and wacky noises. Physical humor, also referred to as slapstick, uses over-the-top violence to comic effect. Characters stumble, fall, or get bonked on the head but quickly recover. Self-deprecating humor is also common; characters make jokes at their own expense. They mock their own looks, abilities, or superpowers for laughs.

*One-Punch Man* combines many forms of humor. The story itself can be classified as a parody; parodies imitate a specific genre while using comic exaggeration to ridicule the style. Saitama utilizes slapstick and self-deprecating jokes. He also uses deadpan humor, delivering funny lines in a matter-of-fact way, with a normal voice and little change of expression.

The mangaka One became an idol of the webcomic world on the basis of the success of *One-Punch Man*. He followed up this accomplishment with the creation of a new manga called *Mob Psycho 100*. The name itself is a joke. It is not about the organized crime syndicate known as the Mob; instead, the story follows Shigeo Kageyama, a timid eighth-grader whose nickname is Mob. And he is not a psycho but a powerful psychic. He can use his gift to destroy evil spirits, malicious psychics, and other supernatural fiends. Like Saitama, Mob is socially awkward and

The protagonist of One Punch Man, whose real name is Saitama, can defeat any enemy with a single punch.

## A LONG HISTORY OF COMEDY

The roots of manga comedy go back 160 years to when English illustrator Charles Wirgman began publishing a Japanese version of the British humor magazine *Punch*, titled *Japan Punch* in 1862. The cartoons in the magazine lampooned the absurdities of daily life in Tokyo. And Wirgman made light of everyone. Europeans were portrayed as the Japanese saw them—hairy, overweight, and with big noses. Residents of Japan were depicted as puzzled and amazed upon seeing their first bicycle or other Western inventions. Japanese leaders were not spared Wirgman's satirical pen. The pages of *Japan Punch* were filled with cartoons mocking government, politics, religion, and law.

Wirgman's cartoon style came to be known as *Ponchi-e* or "*Punch*-style pictures." And *Japan Punch* provided inspiration to a generation of Japanese artists. A Ponchi-e artist named Kitazawa Rakuten introduced the first serialized Sunday comic strip to Japan in 1902. Entitled *Tagosaku and Mokube Sightseeing in Tokyo*, the strip featured two country bumpkins lost in the big city. The full-color strip ran in the Sunday edition of the popular *Jiji Shimpo*, a nationally distributed newspaper. In 1905 Rakuten founded a weekly color cartoon magazine called *Tokyo Puck*. The satirical cartoons in *Puck* attracted widespread attention, and soon the magazine had a circulation of more than one hundred thousand.

---

average looking. And he is not thrilled by his abilities. Mob can use his mind to hurl objects, bounce around enemies, and create vaporizing death balls, but he would rather not. When pushed too far, he explodes into a death-dealing psychic killing machine. But he fears hurting anyone and suppresses his emotions to avoid conflict.

*Mob Psycho 100* is a parody of the action-adventure genre, and there is plenty of deadpan humor. Almost every fight scene begins with Mob using a flat, toneless voice to advise the bad guy to stand down before he gets hurt. *Mob Psycho 100* makes light of the contrast between Mob's apathetic demeanor and the bad guys that he must fight. In the anime, supervillains laugh manically and shriek and squawk in hilarious streams of amplified gibberish. Bloodshot eyes bug out of characters' heads, clouds of steam shoot from ears, and torrents of liquid flow from noses. As the anime reviewer known as Cauthan writes about the on-screen humor:

*Mob Psycho* is an absolute visual feast, possessing some of the most impressive and expressive animation to date. The animation is full of personality—it's erratic, sketchy, and wild. The phenomenal action sequences aren't just flashy. They're full of colors, chaos, debris, and style that fully illustrate just how much passion the show has for its presentation. . . . The result is nothing short of a highly emotive, gorgeous, feast for the eyes.[16]

The "feast for the eyes" helped *Mob Psycho 100* receive several Crunchyroll Anime Awards, including Best Action and Best Animation. In 2022 Crunchyroll announced that the third season of *Mob Psycho 100* was in production.

## FUNNY X FAMILY

*Mob Psycho 100* often relies on over-the-top humor to elicit laughs. The equally popular *Spy x Family*, created by mangaka Tatsuya Endo, uses a gentler type of comedy. The manga and anime feature slice-of-life humor that pokes fun at family dynamics and mundane situations at school, work, and home. In *Spy x Family* this style of comedy is used to lighten what would otherwise be a dramatic tale of intrigue, spying, and assassination.

*Spy x Family* follows a world-class spy known as Twilight who uses the alias Loid Forger. He is on a mission to save the world from conflict between two superpower nations. Loid needs to get married and adopt a child to provide cover for his assignment. He finds an adorable girl named Anya at an orphanage. Loid is unaware that six-year-old Anya is a telepath who can read people's thoughts. Loid marries a woman named Yor Briar who, unknown to Loid, works as a professional assassin called the Thorn Princess. The family also as a pet, a Great Pyrenees dog

> "*Mob Psycho* is an absolute visual feast, possessing some of the most impressive and expressive animation to date. The animation is full of personality—it's erratic, sketchy, and wild."[16]
>
> —Cauthan, anime reviewer

*In* Spy x Family, *a world-class spy known as Twilight gets married and adopts a daughter as part of his cover for his assignment, which is to save the world from conflict between two superpower nations.*

named Bond. Because of her telepathic abilities, Anya can communicate with the dog, who has the ability to see into the future.

Much of the humor in *Spy x Family* is delivered by Anya, who is the only one who knows what is really going on with her dysfunctional family. The story also uses visual humor for laughs. Anya has super cute pink floppy hair, and she expresses her feelings with dumbstruck, horrified, or smug facial expressions that have made her a fan favorite. And as reviewer Allyson Johnson writes, Anya's unique personality traits have also helped boost her popularity:

> The aspect that's captured the internet's heart—rightly so—is the character Anya. . . . Despite being the "gifted" child with secret powers, that is as far as her abilities go. She isn't a genius, she isn't at all competent in sports . . . , and even her ability to read minds has landed her with greater confusion than any sort of insight. The fact that they've decided to make this character frankly kind of dumb . . . [sets] the stage for some of the funniest moments on the show, both in terms of how her confusion is visualized in expressive character design but also in the miscommunication and comedy of errors that befall her and her adopted family because of it.[17]

## SO BAD IT'S GOOD

Comedy has become a very prominent element of shonen manga and anime. Humor provides relief from some of the overly dramatic and depressing plot points in stories. But sometimes the humor in a series is unintentional. Reviewers refer to this category as "so bad it's good." And several anime series have become internet famous for dumb dialogue, stupid setups, and awful animation. Comics journalist Melissa Issaoun explains:

> Given how many [anime] get produced and released into the world every year, it can sometimes happen that their intentions go off track and create chaotic, confusing shows. These often gain infamy within the community and become well-loved for the beautiful trainwrecks they are. Comedic value can be found in many of these anime, and some are even considered worth watching simply to see the monstrous masterpieces unwittingly created by the anime industry.[18]

## DARK COMEDY

Humor can be found in many genres of manga and anime, including action, fantasy, sci-fi, and horror. Sometimes creators use a type of humor called dark comedy to produce laughs when characters are in desperate or dangerous situations. Dark comedy is also known as black humor or gallows humor. Writers use it when they want to make light of serious or painful subjects, including injuries, crime, disasters, and death. A story with good dark comedy illuminates the absurdity of a horrible situation, allowing viewers to share the hero's bravery while laughing in the face of tragedy. As anime reviewer Anna Lindwasser writes:

Humor can be a fantastic coping mechanism for dealing with the most painful parts of life. It may seem distasteful to crack jokes about depressed teachers, socially isolated teenagers, or souls who get tortured in Hell, but sometimes that's the only way to cope. Anime with dark humor isn't for the faint of heart or the easily offended—but if you're into it, it's some of the best comedy out there.

Anna Lindwasser, "15 Anime with Insanely Dark Humor," Ranker, September 26, 2022. www.ranker.com.

---

The horror subgenre is home to some anime that falls into the so-bad-it's-good category. Animators try to grab the viewers' attention by inserting scenes of shocking violence. But that technique can backfire when the mayhem is so exaggerated that viewers do not wince but laugh out loud instead. That is how many view the 2011 supernatural horror anime *Blood-C*. The story is about a girl named Saya who protects her village by fighting off monsters that include a giant town-devouring rabbit suitably named Bunny. Some found the convoluted plot hard to follow, and the beasts, which were supposed to be frightening, elicited laughter instead. Anime blogger Angelo Delos Trinos notes, "*Blood-C* had a lot of problems, one of which was its horror or the lack thereof. . . . The anime's story was so muddled that it failed to scare anyone, and . . . many of the kills and horror elements were just unintentionally hilarious."[19]

> "*Blood-C* had a lot of problems. . . . The anime's story was so muddled that it failed to scare anyone, and . . . many of the kills and horror elements were just unintentionally hilarious."[19]
>
> —Angelo Delos Trinos, anime blogger

Whatever viewers might think of the humor in *Blood-C*, the anime was popular enough that it was adapted into three animated films and a stage play that were less bloody, and less funny, than the original series. The anime series *Ghost Stories*, which follows a group of kids trying to protect their town from malevolent ghosts, never produced any spin-offs. The original twenty episodes, released in 2000, were seen as a financial and critical flop. This prompted the producers to turned *Ghost Stories* over to an American distributor that was hired to dub the story in English. The team in charge of the translation completely changed the dialogue. While keeping the overall basics of the story, the writers added new lines that included dark humor, pop cultural references, and even jokes about the low quality of the animation.

The director put in charge of the translation, Steven Foster, is a fan of the extremely popular, and often offensive, American animated TV comedy *South Park*. As Foster wrote on his blog,

*Steven Foster, who was in charge of creating an English translation of* Ghost Stories, *is a fan of the extremely popular American animated television comedy* South Park *(pictured).*

"I'm probably best known for the cult hit 'Ghost Stories,' a once ho-hum kids' show I transformed into 'the South Park of anime' and 'a comedy for the ages' and, according to [more than 4 million] people on YouTube, the best dub ever produced.'"[20]

## ANIMATION HORRORS

While silly plots and dialogue can evoke laughs sometimes, some anime fails are blamed on technological mishaps. The cop-thriller anime *Ex-Arm* quickly became infamous for its bad CGI after it debuted on Crunchyroll in 2021. Animators placed hand-drawn characters in the same frame as those generated by computers. While the hand animation looks flat, toneless, and slightly out of focus, the CGI characters are sharp and three-dimensional. Reviewer Anthony Gramuglia adds that character mouth movements look weird. "Whenever characters speak, their bottom jaw moves but their lips remain frozen in place" he says. "This results in a profoundly uncanny effect, in which faces remain stuck and lifeless no matter the situation."[21]

*Ex-Arm* received an unusually low 1.8 rating (out of 10) by Crunchyroll viewers. Some thought *Ex-Arm* was so bad, and accidentally funny, that they created YouTube videos to highlight the poor production. While some laughed, others cringed, proving that humor is a matter of personal taste. But manga and anime are created for pure entertainment value, and people love to laugh. Whether the humor is intentional or a result of bad production, series ranging from *One-Punch Man* to *Ex-Arm* are created to help people escape from the daily grind. Some stories make fans laugh until they cry, while others just produce a few chuckles. While horror, fantasy, action, and sci-fi series can feature scenes of drama and heartbreak, the laugh breaks provide a release for fans when they become too emotionally engaged in the story.

## CHAPTER FOUR

# FANTASY WORLDS AND MAGIC GIRLS

Renowned filmmaker Steven Spielberg became a huge fan of anime in the late 1970s at a time when few Americans had heard of Japanese animation. Spielberg came to love anime after viewing *The Castle of Cagliostro* in 1979. The feature-length adventure anime was written and directed by Hayao Miyazaki. Spielberg was so amazed that he financed Miyazaki's second feature-length fantasy animation, *Nausicaä of the Valley of the Wind*, released in 1984. The anime tells the tale of a warrior princess named Nausicaä who lives in a small kingdom named Valley of the Wind. Blogger Ren Scateni says of the heroine, "Nausicaä is an incredibly complex and nuanced character. She is half-Disney princess, demonstrating piety and a close bond with nature, but she also displays traits more commonly associated with male protagonists . . . [such as taking] vengeance on a bunch of soldiers who attacked her village."[22]

> "Nausicaä is an incredibly complex and nuanced character. She is half-Disney princess . . . but she also displays traits more commonly associated with male protagonists."[22]
>
> —Ren Scateni, blogger

*Nausicaä of the Valley of the Wind* is set in a postapocalyptic Earth, where a toxic fungus and giant insects are threatening humanity. The flora and fauna in the Valley of the Wind evoke visions of Earth millions of years in the future,

*The fantasy animation* Nausicaä of the Valley of the Wind *depicts a postapocalyptic earth, with images of flora and fauna that evoke visions of the world millions of years in the future.*

when jungles and pastoral fields have reclaimed the land but environmental calamity has created places with names such as the Acid Lake and the Sea of Decay.

## BUILDING FANTASY WORLDS

Miyazaki is revered for his ability to create epic fantasy worlds. This process, known as world building, requires writers, artists, and animators to create fictional settings filled with finely detailed people, animals, plants, and geographic features. World builders invent unique clothing, machines, buildings, magical systems, governments, animals, and creatures such as space aliens and supernatural monsters. The worlds might exist as future or past versions of Earth or as totally unique environments.

One subgenre of such fantasy is known as *isekai*. The Japanese word translates as "different world" or "otherworld." In isekai stories, protagonists are somehow transported from their daily lives in the so-called real world to a fantasy land that might exist in a virtual world or a parallel dimension. Isekai protagonists are usually on some type of quest or mission that must be accomplished to save themselves or others. Anime blogger Levana Chester-Londt explains that isekai stories are popular because they "will leave the audience feeling as if they have entered into Another World right alongside the protagonist."[23]

The popular anime series *Re: Zero—Starting Life in Another World* is an isekai narrative. The story, often referred to simply as *Re: Zero*, features a seventeen-year-old protagonist named Subaru Natsuki. Subaru's voyage to a different world begins while he is paging through manga magazines in a convenience store. He is suddenly transported to the Kingdom of Lugunica, which resembles a medieval European city. But Lugunica is populated by an assortment of elves, cat-people, lizard-people, and regular humans. Their carriages are pulled by dinosaurs.

> "[Isekai stories] will leave the audience feeling as if they have entered into Another World right alongside the protagonist."[23]
>
> —Levana Chester-Londt, anime blogger

As the story unfolds, Subaru is often confused. As a manga fan he is familiar with the isekai trope, in which protagonists gain superpowers when they enter a parallel universe, but Subaru is weak and unable to fight back when accosted by street urchins who try to rob him. He is saved from the robbers by Emilia, a beautiful elfish girl with supernatural powers. Emilia has silver hair and purple eyes and is followed by a magical talking cat that can read people's minds and seriously harm enemies if need be. Emilia saves Subaru on her way to complete another mission: finding a special insignia that was stolen from her. Emilia needs the insignia to become the queen of Lugunica.

Subaru decides to repay Emilia's kindness by helping her. He locates the insignia in a run-down house on the poor side of town but is murdered by a shadowy assassin. Fans need not worry, however. Subaru wakes up to find himself at the beginning of his otherworldly journey to Lugunica. He realizes that he is stuck in a time loop. He tries to make sense of the situation by returning to the place where he was killed. Subaru ends up dead once

## MASTER OF FANTASY HAYAO MIYAZAKI

Hayao Miyazaki is renowned throughout the world as one of the greatest artists, animators, and writers in manga and anime history. Following the success of the dark fantasy *Nausicaä of the Valley of the Wind* in 1984, Miyazaki founded Studio Ghibli to produce animated features. Since that time the studio has produced several award-winning anime in the fantasy genre that were written and directed by Miyazaki. The historical fantasy *Princess Mononoke* (1997) is about a kingdom where gods of the forest struggle against humans who consume too many resources. Another legendary Miyazaki fantasy, *Spirited Away*, won the Academy Award for Best Animated Feature in 2001. More recent Studio Ghibli fantasy productions include *The Tale of the Princess Kaguya* (2013) and *Earwig and the Witch* (2022).

Miyazaki was eighty-one years old in 2022 and was still hard at work. He dislikes computer animation and continues to draw by hand, saying, "I believe that the tool of the animator is the pencil." Miyazaki's latest work, described as "a fantasy on a grand scale," is an anime adaptation of the 1937 novel *How Do You Live*. The animated feature, scheduled for release in 2023, will doubtless be entertaining anime fans for decades to come.

Quoted in Ligaya Mishan, "Hayao Miyazaki Prepares to Cast One Last Spell," *New York Times*, November 23, 2021. www.nytimes.com.

again. The story carries on for more than fifty episodes as Subaru relives past events, tangles with various enemies, gets killed, and reawakens. Over time, he works to get stronger while increasing his magical powers so he can help Emilia on her quest.

*Re: Zero* has many common tropes found in the fantasy genre. The story features an awkward, clueless protagonist trapped in a world he cannot comprehend. He meets a beautiful magical girl with a supernatural talking pet. And of course, there are numerous fight scenes and screen-shaking explosions.

*Re: Zero* was the most-watched series on Crunchyroll in 2016 because the anime goes beyond typical fantasy clichés. Emilia has a mysterious connection to the evilest witch in Lugunica history. This keeps viewers guessing about her true nature. And Subaru, who is initially overwhelmed by his situation, learns and grows in many ways that fans can understand. As a blogger known as mr.animereviewer explains:

[Subaru] is surprisingly resourceful and intelligent, but not a genius. He is quick to realize the extent of his situation and begin to work on a solution. He addresses most of his problems in a very thoughtful way which feels very real. . . . Although he is the main character of the anime, he is clearly not the main character of the world he is in. The world moves without him and will walk right over him. It's actually like our world now that I think about it.[24]

Unlike most anime series, *Re: Zero* did not originate from a manga. The story was adapted from a light novel written by Tappei Nagatsuki. Light novels with around two hundred pages are created primarily for Japanese high school students. Nagatsuki started writing *Re: Zero* for fun in 2012. He released the first volumes for free on the internet. The story was well received, which inspired Nagatsuki to continue writing. As of 2023 he had written thirty-one volumes of *Re: Zero*, along with five side-story volumes and seven short-story collections. Over 4.6 million copies of the light novels are in print. The first three volumes were adapted to manga during 2014 to 2020, while new anime were released during 2016 to 2021. *Re: Zero* has also been developed into video games, a virtual reality app, and a role-playing mobile game.

## GIRLS WITH PARANORMAL POWERS

Subaru is the main protagonist in *Re: Zero*, while Emilia plays a secondary role. But fantasy stories in the magical girl subgenre place females with supernatural powers at the center of the story. In Japan these individuals are referred to as *mahou shoujo* ("magical girl") or *majokko* ("witch girl").

Protagonists in the magical girl subgenre are usually normal schoolgirls, but they are somehow able to harness fantastic paranormal powers from a magical object such as a pendant, wand, or ribbon. They are often thrust into dire situations, and they must use their magic to ward off evil or protect Earth. Magical girls often possess secret identities, and they always seem to have a powerful talking pet as a sidekick.

There are a few kinds of magical girls commonly found in manga and anime. The cute sorceress type would rather ignore her powers so she can hang out with her friends and flirt with boys. The magical girl warrior is a superhero who takes on supernatural enemies. Other stories might feature magical girl music idols or subversive bad-girl witches who use dark magic to create mayhem.

Almost all manga and anime fans have heard of the famous 1992 anime series *Sailor Moon*, which introduced the magical girl subgenre to the world. *Sailor Moon* was created by Naoko Takeuchi. While growing up in the 1970s, Takeuchi—like all schoolgirls in Japan—wore a sailor-style school uniform. While working as a mangaka in the early 1990s, Takeuchi decided she wanted to create a manga about crime fighters in outer space. In 1991 her ideas came together in the manga *Pretty Soldier Sailor Moon*, or simply *Sailor Moon*.

The series follows a schoolgirl named Usagi Tsukino, who transforms into a girl with magical powers called Sailor Moon. She assembles a team, the Sailor Guardians, who can transform from normal schoolgirls into crime-fighting heroes with supernatural powers. Sailor Moon, Sailor Venus, Sailor Mercury, Sailor Jupiter, and the others battle dark forces from outer space, monsters from another dimension, and wicked life-forms bent on destroying the universe.

*Sailor Moon*, serialized until 1997, became one of the most popular manga of all time. In 1997 the English version of *Sailor Moon* appeared in the United States, where it quickly became the best-selling shojo manga. *Sailor Moon* fans celebrated the twentieth anniversary of the franchise in 2012. By that time the manga had sold over 35 million copies in fifty countries.

The *Sailor Moon* anime began airing in 1992 only a month after the first issue of the manga was published. While the animation studio planned to produce the series for only six months,

*The anime series* Sailor Moon, *created by Naoko Takeuchi, introduced the magical girl subgenre to the world.*

the runaway success of the manga led the studio to create two hundred episodes, which aired over five years. Beginning in 1993 the *Sailor Moon* anime could be seen across Asia and Europe. In 1995 the *Sailor Moon* anime began airing in the United States.

### WITCHES AND SUPER CATS

In 2022 *Sailor Moon* was still topping fan favorite lists, and many magical girl stories followed. *Little Witch Academia*, created by Yoh Yoshinari, is a magical girl story set in a Harry Potter–like world. When a girl with no paranormal powers named Akko goes to the Luna Nova Magical Academy, she discovers an enchanted artifact. This sets Akko on a quest to reintroduce the beauty of magic to a world that is too busy to care.

The manga and anime series *Tokyo Mew Mew*, written by Reiko Yoshida and illustrated by Mia Ikumi, is a mash-up of tropes; Ichigo is a girl who accidently ends up with wild leopard cat DNA in

## THE DARK FANTASY OF DEMON SLAYER

Dark fantasy stories often feature quests that include extended martial arts battles, horrific monsters, and nonstop mayhem. Some of the most successful manga and anime ever created are categorized as dark fantasy. And one of the most popular in the genre, *Demon Slayer: Kimetsu no Yaiba*, created by Koyoharu Gotouge, sold more than 150 million copies in a record-setting four years in 2016 to 2020. A successful anime series and several movies followed.

*Demon Slayer* follows a noble orphaned teenager named Tanjiro Kamado who becomes a demon slayer to avenge the slaughter of his family. Dark fantasies often feature vile and malicious villains who are horrible beyond belief. In *Demon Slayer* that role is embodied in the bloodthirsty Demon King Muzan Kibutsuji. The Demon King kills Tanjiro's family but spares his little sister, Nezuko, after turning her into a demon. While most demons are unfeeling beasts, Nezuko retains her human emotions. However, she must wear a bamboo gag over her mouth to restrain her urge to slaughter humans. Tanjiro must find a cure for her. The heart-wrenching relationship between Tanjiro and Nezuko, along with the high-stakes battles and bloody action scenes, helped make *Demon Slayer* a best-selling dark fantasy masterpiece.

---

her body after an earthquake. (The leopard cat is an endangered small, wild cat that resembles a leopard.) Mia discovers that she can transform into Mew Ichigo, a powerful superhero with leopard-like powers. Mew Ichigo organizes a group of five girls who, during the earthquake, had their DNA merged with other endangered animals, including a dolphin and gray wolf. They form the Mew Mews, who fight invading space aliens while finding romance.

## FIGHTING FEMALE PROTAGONISTS

There is no shortage of magical girl stories filled with cute crime fighters. But some strong female leads in the fantasy genre do not follow the typical tropes. One of the most beloved protagonists, Mikasa Ackerman, stars in *Attack on Titan*, created by mangaka Hajime Isayama.

*Attack on Titan* falls into the dark fantasy genre; the colors are muted, the mood is gloomy, the characters face a catalog of horrors. This is meant to provide viewers with a relentless sense of dread. The story is set in a postapocalyptic world where deformed 50-foot-tall (15 m) giants called Titans stalk and eat people. Humans live in medieval cities surrounded by three enormous walls that keep out the people eaters. But one of the outer walls is breached by a Titan colossus that is even bigger than the others. So begins the tale of Mikasa and her childhood friend—the male protagonist Eren Yeager. They are on a mission to eradicate all the Titans.

Mikasa is unlike many female characters seen in fantasy series. She is a skilled solider with strong values, and she is often tougher and braver than the men around her. Her perilous choice

*Some strong female leads in the fantasy genre, such as* Attack on Titan *protagonist Mikasa Ackerman (shown), are unlike many female characters in fantasy series.*

> "[*Attack on Titan*] is jam-packed with fast-paced episodes; head-spinning plot twists that will shock even *Game of Throne[s]* enthusiasts."[25]
>
> —Olivia Pettman, reviewer

to eliminate Titans and save humanity takes fans on a suspense-filled death-defying quest. Reviewer Olivia Pettman insists, "This anime is jam-packed with fast-paced episodes; head-spinning plot twists that will shock even *Game of Throne[s]* enthusiasts; and intricately designed characters. . . . The men [are] more emotional than the women. It's a great series promoting women power."[25]

*Attack on Titan* is one of the most popular series created in the past decade. The manga, which was serialized from 2009 to 2021, has sold over 110 million tankōbon. The eighty-seven-episode, four-season anime ran from 2014 to 2022. According to Parrot Analytics, the fourth-season series finale of *Attack on Titan* was the most popular television show in the United States on the day it was released. The show also broke the Guinness World Record for the most in-demand anime TV show in history. In 2022 the Crunchyroll Anime Awards named the first episode of the final season of *Attack on Titan* Anime of the Year.

*Attack on Titan* proves that the public's love for the fantasy genre is long running and durable. The genre allows people to see themselves in heroic figures who are often regular people doing remarkable things. The world-building includes fantastic forests, incredible kingdoms, moral quests, mortal battles, monsters, and magic. While fantasy can be suspenseful and violent at times, stories also provide messages about teamwork, friendship, and the power of perseverance. Above all, the fantasy genre allows fans to escape their daily lives and travel to exciting worlds where cats can talk and normal kids have mystical powers that allow them to vanquish even the most powerful enemies.

# CHAPTER FIVE

# ACTION AND ADVENTURE

It is not often that someone creates a manga that defines an entire genre. But mangaka Eiichiro Oda accomplished that feat with the adventure series *One Piece*. The epic story, launched in 1997, features world-spanning adventures that fill more than one thousand chapters. *One Piece* chronicles the escapades of a seventeen-year-old boy named Monkey D. Luffy and his gang called the Straw Hat Pirates.

Like characters in almost every adventure manga, Luffy is on a quest. He is searching to find a mythical treasure called One Piece that would allow him to become King of the Pirates. The One Piece treasure contains the wealth of the entire world, and every pirate is fighting to obtain it. The action unfolds on a globe-spanning ocean route called the Grand Line. No adventure story would be complete without the hero facing numerous hazards, and the Grand Line is teeming with dangers. It is commonly referred to as the Pirates' Graveyard because the currents and weather are erratic. Numerous islands along the Grand Line create magnetic waves that make the sea dangerous and unpredictable.

While fighting to keep their ship on course, Luffy and the Straw Hat Pirates face off against a mind-bending assortment of dangerous characters, including pirate gangs, giants, massive ship-destroying water creatures called sea

> "The beauty of [*One Piece*] resides in its contradictions: exaggerated, cartoon-like graphics present a complicated pirate world with its own myths, customs, and varied characters."[26]
>
> —Manish Prabhakar Singh, Japanese culture scholar

kings, and fish-human hybrids called merfolk. The World Government that rules the Grand Line is another source of peril. This corrupt organization destroys its enemies using secret agents, assassins, and powerful pirates known as the Seven Warlords of the Sea. As Japanese culture scholar Manish Prabhakar Singh writes, "The beauty of [*One Piece*] resides in its contradictions: exaggerated, cartoon-like graphics present a complicated pirate world with its own myths, customs, and varied characters."[26]

Manga and anime in the adventure genre often feature a similar story arc. Obstacles must always be overcome for the protagonist to achieve his or her primary goal. Supernatural beasts, natural disasters, nasty humans, and other hurdles slow the hero's progress to the distant horizon where the treasure lies. And protagonists always have a special ability that allows them to overcome their enemies. Luffy came about his superpower by accident. He ate a magical food called Devil Fruit that gives consumers various formidable traits. When Luffy eats the magical fruit, he turns into a rubber man; he can stretch his limbs, neck, and torso to deliver kicks, punches, head butts, and other defensive maneuvers. But as any fan of adventure manga knows, superpowers often come with limitations. While the Devil Fruit gives Luffy incredible strength, energy, and elasticity, it takes away his ability to swim; he loses his powers when submerged in water. This is a great disadvantage in the *One Piece* world, which consists mostly of oceans. In addition, Luffy is not the only character who eats Devil Fruit. His enemies also consume the superfood, and each is affected differently. Some turn into murderous crows, while others can transform their bodies into ice.

### INFLUENTIAL AND AMAZING

It is no exaggeration to say that nearly every adventure manga and anime series created in the twenty-first century has been influenced by *One Piece*. According to Singh, "The series is not only recognized for its action sequences but also for its rich story and distinctive character designs. *One Piece* experiments with remarkable character and physical transformations, fantastic combat styles, and supernatural powers as a classic shōnen-manga."[27]

The complex world of *One Piece* mixes humor, puns, and Luffy's innocent idealism with shocking real-world-type events that include bloody combat, slavery, government corruption, and mass murder. The story has sixty separate characters, each with their own biography that includes personality traits, physical attributes, superpowers, and battle histories. These are spelled out in more than six thousand articles on the *One Piece* fandom wiki page. The site covers every location, organization, plant, food, and technology created by Oda.

*The adventure series* One Piece *chronicles the adventures of a seventeen-year-old boy named Monkey D. Luffy (pictured) and his gang called the Straw Hat Pirates.*

Oda was still writing and drawing *One Piece* in 2023, when the 104 tankōbon volumes had sold nearly 517 million copies. These figures make *One Piece* the best-selling single-author comic ever created, according to Guinness World Records. And the manga generated an equally successful twenty-season anime series with over 1,040 episodes. The *One Piece* franchise also includes fourteen feature-length animated films and at least fifty-six video games. Oda says he plans to wrap up his decade-spanning adventure blockbuster in 2025.

## MARTIAL ARTS ACTION

With its seafaring pirates and never-ending global escapades, adventure is the focus of *One Piece*. Manga and anime that emphasize adrenaline-pumping swordplay, hand-to-hand combat, gunfights, and explosions are categorized as action stories. Characters in action anime constantly struggle against much stronger foes, and the fight scenes tend to follow specific patterns. As the legendary martial artist Bruce Lee put it, "An action scene is essentially a small play."[28] What Lee meant is that every battle scene has a beginning, middle, and end, each with similar features. In the beginning the protagonist is fighting with little hope against a skilled opponent or small army. In the middle of a typical action scene, the hero appears to be down for the count, beaten and nearly dead. But in the end the character emerges bruised and battered but victorious, at least until the next fight takes place and the small action play repeats itself.

> "An action scene is essentially a small play."[28]
>
> —Bruce Lee, martial arts legend

Lee was a movie star who is credited with popularizing martial arts movies in the 1970s. Since that time martial arts manga and anime have become an essential subgenre of the action category. These stories can trace their roots back to the ancient Japanese samurai tradition that emerged in the late twelfth century. The samurai upheld a strict code, called Bushido, or "the Way of the Warrior," which required self-sacrifice, loyalty, and fair play even in battle.

## HIGH SCHOOL MARTIAL ARTISTS

Some of the most popular manga and anime series revolve around martial arts. Fans love this subgenre because it features competitions and power struggles highlighted by realistic fight scenes featuring samurai and ninja warriors. And in many stories, martial arts combat occurs in or around high schools. *The God of High School*, created by South Korean artist Yongje Park, follows a seventeen-year-old martial artist named Mori Jin who battles other schoolkids to be named World Tournament Champion. Mori practices karate, tae kwon do, and other martial arts as he spins, jumps, and kicks his way through realistic fight scenes.

High school martial arts action stories often incorporate supernatural elements. *Jujutsu Kaisen*, created by Gege Akutami, features Yuji Itadori, an unusually strong high school kid. Yuji is a member of his high school Occult Club, which accidentally attracts curses to his school. Yuji is consumed by Cursed Energy and must join a secret group called the Jujutsu Sorcerers to learn to control his powers. The fate of the world depends on Yuji's strength and fighting abilities. *Jujutsu Kaisen* was the second-most watched anime on Crunchyroll in 2022. Reviewers hailed the show as a fresh take on a common subgenre.

The type of Japanese warrior known as a ninja does not follow the Bushido code. Ninjas use sabotage, espionage, and assassination as well as open combat to achieve their goals. They are masters of disguise, expert fighters, and excessively violent. This makes ninjas perfect heroes and villains for shonen manga and anime, from the classic *Dragon Ball* to the latest blockbuster *Jujutsu Kaisen*.

## NINJA NARUTO

The martial arts subgenre is responsible for some of the best-selling manga in history, including the beloved blockbuster *Naruto*. The manga, written and illustrated by Masashi Kishimoto from 1999 to 2015, follows a young, troubled ninja fighter named Naruto Uzumaki. The incredibly complex story, which sold over 250 million tankōbon volumes, develops over 453 manga chapters and 720 anime episodes produced from 2002 to 2017.

The epic story of Naruto is told in two parts. Part one takes place when Naruto is in his preteen years; part two follows the character as a teen. Like hundreds of other manga and anime characters, Naruto is an orphan on a quest. Naruto hopes to become the strongest ninja in his village, Konoha. But Naruto is shunned by the people of Konoha because he carries in his body the spirit of the beastly town-destroying fox named Nine-Tails.

Naruto joins the crime-fighting Team 7 and learns to use supernatural ninja powers to battle evil. The story features a powerful group of villains, the Akatsuki, made up of rebels, outlaws, and outcasts. While battling the Akatsuki, Naruto has many opportunities to display his fighting skills. Anime journalist De'Angelo Epps writes, "*Naruto* has some of the most enjoyable and creative fights in the medium due to its great concepts . . . some awesome choreography . . . [and] some sick martial-arts-inspired battles."[29]

*The protagonist of the blockbuster manga* Naruto, *a troubled teenager named Naruto Uzumaki (pictured), hopes to become the strongest ninja in his village.*

*Naruto* is a fan favorite and one of the most entertaining action series. But there are plenty of common tropes used in the lengthy, winding story. Like many action heroes, Naruto often has flashbacks to traumatic events in his life. These glimpses into Naruto's previous life help refresh viewers' memories about events in past episodes while providing a little bit of calm between battle scenes. Another common action cliché is known as talking the enemy to death. Before a battle, a protagonist will make jokes and try to prevent the fight by employing diplomacy, empathy, and reason. When Naruto utilizes this trope, it is called "talk jutsu." Naruto's talk jutsu is the source of numerous memes posted on social media.

> "*Naruto* has some of the most enjoyable and creative fights in the medium due to its great concepts . . . some awesome choreography . . . [and] some sick martial-arts-inspired battles."[29]
>
> —De'Angelo Epps, anime journalist

## SUPERHERO SCHOOLS

When Naruto began his long-running quest, he attended a martial arts academy to learn fighting techniques. This placed Naruto in a category with countless other anime characters who attend a training school or high school. And there is a reason schools appear so often in manga and anime stories; according to a study by Statista Research, more than 88 percent of Japanese high school students say they watch anime. This prompts producers to create stories that mirror the daily lives of their young consumers.

Schools play a central role in the lives of Japanese students, and many manga and anime reflect this reality. Students in Japan are required to pass difficult entrance exams before they can attend high school at age fifteen. Manga and anime characters are usually around this age and are often shown studying for tests, worrying about tests, and taking tests. Characters also tend to wear uniforms like those used in the Japanese school system.

The trendy manga and anime *My Hero Academia* feature aspects of the real Japanese school system, but the students in this series are training to be superheroes. Created by Kōhei Horikoshi, *My Hero Academia* focuses on Izuku "Deku" Midoriya. Deku

*The manga titled* My Hero Academia *features aspects of the real Japanese school system, but the students in this series are training to be superheroes.*

lives in a world where 80 percent of the population was born with some sort of superpower, or what the people call a "Quirk." Everyone's Quirk is unique. Depending on how they use their powers, they are classified as either heroes or villains.

Deku was born without a Quirk. But he dreams of achieving the revered celebrity status called Pro Hero. Deku meets with the world's greatest superhero, All Might, who grants him superpowers. This leads Deku to enroll in the prestigious U.A. High School to master his newfound powers. Like many leading manga characters, Deku is a nerdy teenaged misfit. Other characters in *My Hero Academia* feature personality profiles common in action stories. Reviewer Scott Gladstein explains: "Students include: a hyper talented rival of a cool and calm disposition, a prideful rival of insane power who acts kinda villainous, a female student who always teams up with the protagonist but really isn't that useful, and a col-

54

orful cast of other characters who get some [attention] but aren't actually all that important to the series."[30] Gladstein notes other standard character types, including grotesque body-horror villains, a mysterious boss calling the shots from behind the scenes, and a quiet mentor who has an amazing power that is rarely used.

*My Hero Academia* is a critical and commercial success. The manga, serialized from 2014 to 2022, includes 306 chapters. The combined 35 tankōbon volumes have sold over 65 million copies. The first season of the *My Hero Academia* anime premiered in the United States and Japan in 2016. By the time the sixth season was released in 2022, the anime was attracting millions of views on Crunchyroll.

Action and adventure stories do more than show high schoolers facing high-stakes battles. They feature protagonists that kids can relate to while presenting never-ending quests that keep fans coming back for more. Stories show that seemingly impossible goals can be achieved through hard work and dedication. As bloggers Eligijus Sinkunas and Melanie Gervasoni write, "The characters might start off from zero, but by the end of their journey, they're

## DRAGON BALL SUPERHERO TROPES

Since its inception in 1985, Akira Toriyama's *Dragon Ball* series has had an overwhelming influence on the manga and anime industries. The story chronicles the adventures of a kung fu–fighting monkey boy named Son Goku. Action unfolds as Goku finds friends and fights enemies while searching for magical Dragon Balls that can make any wish come true.

The story of Goku features several superhero tropes shared by other popular action characters. Goku is an improbably strong orphan from an alien planet. He faces off against supervillains who seem to get progressively stronger as the series unfolds. Goku has superhero skills seen in many stories; he can fly, throw blasts of energy, and read minds. Still, he feels the need to hide his abilities and keep his identity secret. In the end, though, Goku always saves the day by defeating the villain.

The *Dragon Ball* and *Dragon Ball Z* franchises cover 520 manga chapters, 500 anime episodes, and 20 full-length anime films. And many of the tropes popularized by the series can be found in contemporary stories like *Naruto*, *My Hero Academia*, and *JoJo's Bizarre Adventure*.

not just some random nobody who got lucky—they're someone who fought to gain strength, determination, and courage. We see them grow from humble beginnings into confident leaders who inspire their companions with actions and words."[31]

The same tropes that are found in *My Hero Academia*, *One Piece*, and other stories can be found in almost every action and adventure tale, from classical literature to the latest blockbuster movie. And with some manga and anime series unwinding over several decades and thousands of episodes, few can complain that plots are built around similar themes. Sinkunas and Gervasoni write that most fans do not overanalyze the formulas used by creators; instead, "the excitement for adventure is like catnip for anime fans. We love the thrill of [the] action, the wild ride that comes with watching a story unfold in front of our eyes."[32]

# SOURCE NOTES

## INTRODUCTION: SO MANY CHOICES

1. Nicole Rousmaniere, "8 Manga Genres You Need to Know," British Museum, June 3, 2019. www.britishmuseum.org.
2. Madison Roach, "Anime Is Better than Western Animation," The Breeze, February 21, 2022. www.breezejmu.org.

## CHAPTER ONE: SCI-FI WORLDS OF SPACE AND TECHNOLOGY

3. Charles Solomon, "Happy 80th Birthday, Yoshiyuki Tomino! 'Gundam' Creator Discusses Inspirations & Legacy in Rare Interview," *Animation Magazine*, November 5, 2021. www.animationmagazine.net.
4. Quoted in Van Gogh Alive, "Artists in 60 Seconds: Tezuka Osamu," 2021. www.vangoghgenova.it.
5. Monica Kim, "Can *Cowboy Bebop*'s Creator Make More People Take Anime Seriously?," *The Atlantic*, January 3, 2014. www.theatlantic.com.
6. Quoted in Tyler Aquilina, "The Ballad of *Cowboy Bebop*: How an Oddball Japanese Series Became an Anime Landmark," *Entertainment Weekly*, November 19, 2021. https://ew.com.
7. Arius Raposas, "*Dr. Stone* Review: Science Meets Anime in a Most Practical Fashion and It Works," Medium, March 28, 2021. https://medium.com.

## CHAPTER TWO: ROMANCE, DRAMA, AND FUN

8. Coco Masters, "Something About Shojo," *Time*, August 10, 2006. http://content.time.com.
9. Deb Aoki, "Top Shojo Manga Must-Reads," LiveAbout, January 5, 2019. www.liveabout.com.
10. Callie Cadorniga, "The 'Fruits Basket' Story Is Tragic and Lovely, and the Movie Seeks to Continue the Magic," Distractify, October 29, 2021. www.distractify.com.

11. Kirsty Kawano, "Boys' Love, the Genre That Liberates Japanese Women to Create a World of Their Own," Savvy Tokyo, January 17, 2019. https://savvytokyo.com.
12. Jitendar Canth, "Review for *Kiss Him, Not Me*," MyReviewer.com, 2018. www.myreviewer.com.
13. Sebastian Stoddard, "Sing It Loud! An Intro to the World of Idol Anime," Collider, September 26, 2021. https://collider.com.
14. Raziel Reaper, "Reaper's Reviews," Reel Rundown, March 24, 2022. https://reelrundown.com.

## CHAPTER THREE: PARODIES, SLAPSTICK, AND OTHER COMEDY

15. Rafael Motamayor, "'One Punch Man' Is a Hilarious Anime Parody of Superhero Stories," *SlashFilm* (blog), May 8, 2020. www.slashfilm.com.
16. Cauthan, "Review: *Mob Psycho 100*," *Cauthan Reviews* (blog), September 27, 2016. https://cauthan.wordpress.com.
17. Allyson Johnson, "'Spy x Family' Is as Funny as It Is Charming," Pajiba, June 25, 2022. www.pajiba.com.
18. Melissa Issaoun, "10 Shonen Anime That Were Unintentionally Hilarious," CBR, December 22, 2021. www.cbr.com.
19. Angelo Delos Trinos, "10 Horror Anime Series That Are More Bloody than Scary," CBR, October 21, 2021. www.cbr.com.
20. Quoted in Deshawn Thomas, "Why Everyone Thinks the Cult Classic Anime *Ghost Stories* Bombed in Japan—When It Didn't," *SlashFilm* (blog), November 21, 2022. www.slashfilm.com.
21. Anthony Gramuglia, "*Ex-Arm*'s Animation Is So Bad It Might Be Unintentionally Homophobic," CBR, January 21, 2021. www.cbr.com.

## CHAPTER FOUR: FANTASY WORLDS AND MAGIC GIRLS

22. Ren Scateni, "In This Age of Ecological Crisis, Nausicaä's Message Is More Vital than Ever," Little White Lies, November 25, 2019. https://lwlies.com.
23. Quoted in Patrick Armstrong, "13 Isekai Anime That Have Awesome World Building," Game Rant, November 23, 2022. https://gamerant.com.
24. mr.animereviewer, "*Re Zero* Season 1 Review: At First You Don't Succeed, Die, Die Again," Comic Watch, May 14, 2020. https://comic-watch.com.

25. Olivia Pettman, "*Attack on Titan* Anime Review," Medium, December 29, 2018. https://medium.com.

## CHAPTER FIVE: ACTION AND ADVENTURE

26. Manish Prabhakar Singh, "Odyssey of the Cultural Narrative: Japan's Cultural Representation in Eiichiro Oda's *One Piece*," *Global Media Journal*, Indian Edition, June 2021. https://gmj.manipal.edu.
27. Singh, "Odyssey of the Cultural Narrative."
28. Quoted in Justin Moriarty, "What Makes an Action Anime?," Honey's Anime, May 2, 2019. https://honeysanime.com.
29. De'Angelo Epps, "10 Reasons Why *Naruto* Is the Best of *Shonen Jump*'s Big Three," CBR, February 22, 2020. www.cbr.com.
30. Scott Gladstein, "*My Hero Academia* Review," Medium, June 23, 2017. https://medium.com.
31. Eligijus Sinkunas and Melanie Gervasoni, "Adventure Anime Shows That Will Hook You Right from the Start," Bored Panda, 2022. www.boredpanda.com.
32. Sinkunas and Gervasoni, "Adventure Anime Shows That Will Hook You Right from the Start."

# FOR FURTHER RESEARCH

## BOOKS

Marc Bernabe, *Learn Japanese with Manga*. North Clarendon, VT: Tuttle, 2022.

Hector Garcia, *A Geek in Japan: Discovering the Land of Manga, Anime, Zen, and the Tea Ceremony*. North Clarendon, VT: Tuttle, 2019.

Robert M. Henderson, *Quick Guide to Anime and Manga*. San Diego, CA: ReferencePoint, 2022.

Sho Hinata and Eiichiro Oda, *One Piece: Ace's Story, Vol. 1: Formation of the Spade Pirates*. San Francisco, CA: VIZ Media, 2020.

Stuart A. Kallen, *Art and Artists of Manga*. San Diego, CA: ReferencePoint, 2022.

Kanaya Shunichiro, *A History of Japan in Manga: Samurai, Shoguns and World War II*. North Clarendon, VT: Tuttle, 2023.

## INTERNET RESOURCES

Tyler Aquilina, "The Ballad of *Cowboy Bebop*: How an Oddball Japanese Series Became an Anime Landmark," *Entertainment Weekly*, November 19, 2021. https://ew.com.

Melissa Issaoun, "10 Shonen Anime That Were Unintentionally Hilarious," CBR, December 22, 2021. www.cbr.com.

Kirsty Kawano, "Boys' Love, the Genre That Liberates Japanese Women to Create a World of Their Own," Savvy Tokyo, January 17, 2019. https://savvytokyo.com.

Ligaya Mishan, "Hayao Miyazaki Prepares to Cast One Last Spell," *New York Times Magazine*, November 23, 2021. www.nytimes.com.

Madison Roach, "Anime Is Better than Western Animation," The Breeze, February 21, 2022. www.breezejmu.org.

Zoe Taylor and Matt Thorn, "The Women of the Year 24 Group," *Vrroom!*, Spring 2016. http://nectar.northampton.ac.uk.

## WEBSITES

### Anime News Network
www.animenewsnetwork.com
This is one of the most popular online news sources for anime and manga. The website also provides reviews, press releases, and anime convention reports.

### Anime-Planet
www.anime-planet.com
Registered users of Anime-Planet can stream over forty-five thousand anime episodes, read manga online, find reviews and recommendations, and participate in the site's community forum that covers nearly every topic imaginable.

### CBR
www.cbr.com
This website has tens of thousands of articles on manga, anime, American comics, cartoons, and games, as well as reviews, lists, forums, and news.

### *One Piece*
https://one-piece.com
The English-language version of the *One Piece* website features details about the more than one-thousand-chapter manga drawn by Eiichiro Oda. Readers can learn about the story and the characters, watch anime clips, and shop for related merchandise.

### Tezuka Osamu
https://tezukaosamu.net/en
The official website of Osamu Tezuka features drawings and descriptions about more than two hundred manga and anime series, along with character biographies and other information.

# INDEX

*Note: Boldface page numbers indicate illustrations.*

Academy Award for Best Animated Feature, 40
action/adventure genre
 martial arts subgenre, 50–55
 quests in, 47–50, **49**
 standard characters, 54–55
*Akira*, 4, **6**
Akko (fictional character), 43
Akutami, Gege, 51
All Might (fictional character), 54
American western cowboy genre, 13
Amuro Ray (fictional character), 8
Angelo Delos Trinos, 34
anime
 early, 10–11
 elements common to, 6–7
 manga and, 5
 popularity in US of, 7
 schools in, 53
 shown during Gay Pride Month, 23
 Studio Ghibli and, 40
 visuals
  CGI effects, 8–9
  female mangaka and, 20
  limited animation, 11–12
 *See also* specific genres
Anya (fictional character), 31–33, **32**
Aoki, Deb, 18
*Astro Boy* (television program), 11–12, **12**
*Attack on Titan* (Isayama), 23, 44–46, **45**

*Berserk*, 5
black humor subgenre, 34
*Blood-C*, 34–35
Boichi, 14, 15
Bond (fictional character), 31–32
Boss Borot (fictional character), 11
Bunny (fictional character), 34–35

Bushido, 50–51

Cadorniga, Callie, 18
Canth, Jitendar, 23
Cartoon Network, 13
Cauthan, 30–31
Chester-Londt, Levana, 39
*City of Blank* (66), 15
Clements, Jonathan, 13
comedy. *See* humor genre
computer-generated imagery (CGI) software, 8–9, 36
*Cowboy Bebop* (Watanabe), 12–13, 14, **14**, 16
Crunchyroll
 Anime Awards, 31, 46
 *Cowboy Bebop* on, 13
 *Ex-Arm* on, 36
 *Fruits Basket* on, 18
 *Jujutsu Kaisen* on, 51
 *Kiss Him, Not Me* on, 22
 *Mob Psycho 100* on, 31
 Movie Night, 8
 *My Hero Academia* on, 55
 *One-Punch Man* on, 28
 programming on, 7
 *Re: Zero* on, 40
 *Skip Beat!* on, 25
 Top 25 Best Anime of the 2010s, 16
 *Zombie Land Saga* on, 26
*Cucuruz Doan's Island* (Tomino), 8–9

dark comedy/humor subgenre, 34
dark fantasy subgenre, 44
Deku (fictional character), 53–54, **54**
Demon King Muzan Kibutsuji (fictional character), 44
*Demon Slayer: Kimetsu no Yaiba* (Gotouge), 44
Dick, Philip K., 4
*Do Androids Dream of Electric Sheep* (Dick), 4
Doraemon, 5
*Dr. Stone* (Inagaki and Boichi), 14–16
*Dragon Ball* series (Toriyama), 51, 55
*Dragon Ball Z*, 5, 55

*Duty After School* (Il-Kwon), 15

*Earwig and the Witch* (Miyazaki), 40
Emilia (fictional character), 39, 40, 41
*Emma: A Victorian Romance* (Mori), **21**, 21–22
Endo, Tatsuya, 31
Epps, De'Angelo, 52
Eren Yeager (fictional character), 45
*Ex-Arm*, 36
eyes, 12, 20

fantasy genre
 Miyazaki and, 37–38, **38**
 subgenres
  dark, 44
  historical, 40
  isekai ("different/other world"), 38–41, **38**
  magical girl, 41–44, **43**
film noir genre, 13
flowers, 20
Foster, Steven, 35–36
*Fruits Basket* (Takaya), 17–18, **18**

gallows humor subgenre, 34
gender
 female mangaka and manga changes, 20
 harem and reverse-harem romances, 22–23
 yaoi ("boys' love") fans and, 20–21
genres
 basic facts about, 4
 types of, 5–6
 *See also* specific types
Gervasoni, Melanie, 55–56
*Ghost in the Shell*, 5
*Ghost Stories*, 35–36
*Gigantor*, 11
*Given* (Kizu), 23
Gladstein, Scott, 54–55
*God of High School, The* (Park), 51
Gotouge, Koyoharu, 44
Gramuglia, Anthony, 36

62

Guinness World Records, 46, 50
*Gundam* franchise (Tomino), 8–9, **9**

Hagio, Moto, 19, 20
Hak (fictional character), 22
*Hana to Yume* (*Flowers and Dreams*; Japanese shojo magazine), 17
harem and reverse-harem subgenre, 22–23
*Heart of Thomas, The* (Hagio), 20
Hello Kitty, 5
historical fantasy subgenre, 40
historical romance subgenre, **21**, 21–22
*Honey and Clover*, 6
Horikoshi, Kōhei, 53–55
horror subgenre of humor, 34–36
*How Do You Live* (anime adaptation of), 40
humor genre
  roots of, 30
  subgenres
    black/gallows/dark, 34
    horror, 34–36
    over-the-top, 31–33, **32**
    parody, 28, **29**, 29–31
    "so bad it's good," 33–35
*Hunter x Hunter*, 23

Ichigo (fictional character), 43–44
idol and horror romance subgenre, 25–26
idol romance subgenre, 24–25
Ikeda, Riyoko, 19–20
Ikumi, Mia, 43–44
Il-Kwon, Ha, 15
Inagaki, Riichiro, 14
*Iron Man #28* (Yokoyama), 11
Isayama, Hajime, 23, 44
isekai ("different/other world"), 38–41
Issaoun, Melissa, 33
Izuku "Deku" Midoriya (fictional character), 53–55, **54**

*Japan Punch* (Japanese magazine), 30
*Jiji Shimpo* (Japanese newspaper), 30

Johnson, Allyson, 32–33
*JoJo's Bizarre Adventure*, 55
*josei* manga, 6
*Jujutsu Kaisen* (Akutami), 51
Jump Comics (online magazine), 28
Junko, 22

Kae Serinuma (fictional character), 23
Kawano, Kirsty, 21
Kim, Monica, 13
Kishimoto, Masashi, 51
*Kiss Him, Not Me* (Junko), 22–23
Kizu, Natsuki, 23
*kodomo* manga, 5
Koji Kabuto (fictional character), 11
Kusanagi, Mizuho, 22
Kyoko Mogami (fictional character), 25

Lee, Bruce, 50
LGBTQ+ characters, 23
light novels, 41
Lindwasser, Anna, 34
*Little Witch Academia* (Yoshinari), 43
Loid Forger (fictional character), 31, **32**
*Lore Olympus*, 4
*Loveless*, 6
Luffy (fictional character), 47–49, **49**

magical girl subgenre, 41–44, **43**
*Magi* series, 4
Magnificent 24s, 19, 20
*mahou shoujo* ("magical girl"), 41
*majokko* ("witch girl"), 41
manga
  elements common to, 6–7
  genres of, 5–6
  number of stories printed in Japan annually, 7
  schools in, 53
  visuals in, 20
mangaka
  basic facts about, 5
  female, 19, 20, 22–23
  *See also* specific individuals
manhwa, 15
martial arts subgenre, 50–55
Masters, Coco, 17
*Mazinger Z* (Nagai), 11

mecha, 8, **9**
Mew Ichigo (fictional character), 43–44
*Mighty Atom* (Tezuka), 10–12
Mikasa Ackerman (fictional character), 44–46, **45**
Miyazaki, Hayao, 37, 40
*Mobile Suit Gundam* franchise (Tomino), 8–9
*Mob Psycho 100* (One), 29–31
Monkey D. Luffy (fictional character), 47–49, **49**
Mori, Kaoru, 21
Mori Jin (fictional character), 51
Motamayor, Rafael, 28
Mushi Production, 11
*My Hero Academia* (Horikoshi), 23, 53–55, **54**

Nagai, Go, 11
Nagatsuki, Tappei, 41
Nakamura, Yoshiki, 24–25
*Nakayoshi* (*Best Friend*), 19
*Naruto* (Kishimoto), 51–53, **52**, 55
Naruto Uzumaki (fictional character), 51–53, **52**
*Nausicaä of the Valley of the Wind* (Miyazaki), 37–38, **38**, 40
Netcomics, 15
Netflix, 7, 13
Nezuko (fictional character), 44
ninjas, 51

Oda, Eiichiro, 47, 49–50
One (mangaka), 28
*One Piece* (Oda), 5, 47–50, **49**
*One-Punch Man* (One), 27–28, 29, **29**
*One Thousand and One Nights*, 4
Oscar François de Jarjayes (fictional character), 19
Oshima, Yumiko, 19
*otaku*, 23
*Ouran High School Host Club*, 6
over-the-top humor subgenre, 31–33, **32**

Park, Yongje, 51
parody genre, 28, **29**, 29–31
Parrot Analytics, 46
Pettman, Olivia, 46

63

*Ponchi-e* (*Punch*-style pictures), 30
postapocalyptic sci-fi subgenre, 14–16
*Pretty Soldier Sailor Moon* (Takeuchi), 42–43, **43**
*Princess Mononoke* (Miyazaki), 40
*Psycho-Pass*, 4

Rakuten, Kitazawa, 30
Raposas, Arius, 15
*Re: Zero—Starting Life in Another World*, 39–41
Reaper, Raziel, 25
Roach, Madison, 7
robot sci-fi subgenre, 11
romance genre, **24**
    characters, 19, 23, 26
    subgenres and combo genres, 19
        harem and reverse-harem, 22–23
        historical, **21**, 21–22
        idol, 24–25
        idol and horror, 25–26
        romantic comedy, 17–18, **18**
    themes, 20–21
romantic comedy genre, 17–18, **18**
*Rose of Versailles, The* (Ikeda), 19–20
Rotten Tomatoes, 28
Rousmaniere, Nicole, 5

*Sailor Moon* (Takeuchi), 6, 42–43, **43**
Saitama (fictional character), 27–28, **29**
Sakura Minamoto (fictional character), 25–26
samurai, 50–51
Saya (fictional character), 34–35
Sayaka Yumi (fictional character), 11
Scateni, Ren, 37
sci-fi genre
    early, 11–12, **12**
    subgenres
        film noir, 12–13, **14**
        postapocalyptic, 14–16
        robot, 11
*seinen* manga, 5
self-deprecating humor, 28
Senku Ishigami (fictional character), 14–16

Shima (fictional character), 23
*Shōgo Comic*, 19
shojo manga
    basic facts about, 5–6
    female mangaka and, 19
    *Fruits Basket*, 17–18, **18**
    magazine of, 17
shonen manga, 5–6
Shotaro Fuwa (fictional character), 25
Shotaro Kaneda (fictional character), 11
*Showa 24* (Year 24 Group), 19, 20
Singh, Manish Prabhaka, 48, 49
Sinkunas, Eligijus, 55–56
66 (mangaka), 15
*Skip Beat!* (Nakamura), 24–25
slapstick and self-deprecating humor, 28
"so bad it's good" humor subgenre, 33–35
Solomon, Charles, 8
Son Goku (fictional character), 55
South Korean sci-fi anime, 15
*South Park*, **35**
Spielberg, Steven, 37
*Spirited Away* (Miyazaki), 40
*Spy x Family* (Endo), 31–33, **32**
Statista Research, 53
Stoddard, Sebastian, 25
Straw Hat Pirates, 47–48, **49**
Studio Ghibli, 40
Subaru (fictional character), 39–41

*Tagosaku and Mokube Sightseeing in Tokyo* (Rakuten), 30
Taiju Oki (fictional character), 16
Takahashi, Mizuki, 20
Takaya, Natsuki, 17, 19
Takeuchi, Naoko, 42–43
*Tale of the Princess Kaguya, The* (Miyazaki), 40
"talk jutsu," 53
Tanjiro Kamado (fictional character), 44
*tankōbon*, 16
*Tetsujin 28-gō* (Yokoyama), 11
*Tetsuwan Atomu* (Mighty Atom), 10–12
Tezuka, Osamu, 10–12

Thorn Princess (fictional character), 31
Tohru Honda (fictional character), 17
*Tokyo Mew Mew* (Yoshida and Ikumi), 43–44
*Tokyo Puck* (Japanese magazine), 30
Tomino, Yoshiyuki, **9**, 9–10
Toriyama, Akira, 55
*Transformers, The* (television program), 11
Twilight (fictional character), 31, **32**

United States
    *Attack on Titan* in, 46
    Cartoon Network, 13
    *Fruits Basket* in, 18, **18**
    *Iron Man* exported as *Gigantor* to, 11
    *Mazinger Z* in, 11
    *Mighty Atom* as *Astro Boy* in, 11–12, **12**
    Netflix, 7, 13
    popularity of anime in, 7
    *Sailor Moon* in, 42
    YouTube, 11, 36
    See also Crunchyroll
Usagi Tsukino (fictional character), 42

Watanabe, Shinichirō, 12
webcomics (web manga), 28
Webtoon, 15
Wirgman, Charles, 30
world building, 38, **38**
World Population Review, 7

Yano Research Institute, 20–21
*yaoi* ("boys' love"), 20–21
Yokoyama, Mitsuteru, 11
*Yona of the Dawn* (Kusanagi), 22
Yor Briar (fictional character), 31, **32**
Yoshida, Reiko, 43–44
Yoshinari, Yoh, 43
YouTube, 11, 36
Yuji Itadori (fictional character), 51
Yuki Sohma (fictional character), 17
*yuri* ("girls' love"), 20

*Zombie Land Saga*, 25–26